THE SPACE RACE

A History From Beginning to End

Table of Contents

Introduction

For a relatively short time, the desire to be the first to achieve milestones in space flight and space exploration became a major factor in relations between the United States of America and the Soviet Union. In the 1950s and 1960s, the two superpowers faced each other in a conflict that became known as the Cold War. The threat of nuclear annihilation meant that neither could afford to go to war with the other, and both sought other means of demonstrating the superiority of their systems of government.

This showdown took many forms, but nowhere was the competition more intense or more public than in the attempt to conquer space. In part, this was because both sides saw a military advantage in the domination of space, though they claimed more altruistic motives for their space programs. For several years, both countries forced the pace of space exploration with first one and then the other gaining an advantage. Then, just as suddenly as it had started, the space race was over. Although both countries continued with space missions, these were no longer part of intense competition, and the pace of space exploration slowed dramatically.

This is the dramatic story of the origins of the space race and of the triumphs, failures, and tragedies which it encompassed.

Chapter One

Pioneers of Space Exploration

"The Earth is the cradle of mankind—one cannot remain in the cradle forever."

—Konstantin Tsiolkovsky

The beginnings of scientific interest in space travel can be traced back to two men. Fittingly, given that this is a book about competition between the United States and the Soviet Union, one was American and the other Russian. These two men never met, and each spent most of their life in ignorance of the other, but they separately developed many of the ideas that would lead to the space race and finally take man outside the atmosphere of planet Earth.

Konstantin Tsiolkovsky was one of 18 children born to a poor Polish immigrant family in Tsarist Russia in 1857. An early bout of scarlet fever caused him to become partly deaf, and as a result, he received almost no formal education. When Tsiolkovsky was 16, however, he was able to spend time in Moscow and particularly at the Chertkovskaya Library where for the first time he had unrestricted access to books. Some of the first things he read were the science fiction works of French novelist Jules Verne, including *From the Earth to the Moon* (1865) and *Around the Moon* (1870).

Tsiolkovsky became fascinated by the science behind these fictional accounts of space travel. For example, he rapidly calculated that the cannon used to shoot a spacecraft to the moon in *From the Earth to the Moon* would have produced such crushing acceleration that it would have killed its occupants. By the 1890s, Tsiolkovsky was working as a teacher, but in his spare time, he was writing about space travel. Initially, he tried science fiction, but he quickly discovered that he was more interested in the science than the fiction.

Almost all Tsiolkovsky's ideas were theoretical, but he proved to be incredibly prescient. In 1903, his article "Exploration of the World Space with Reaction Machines" was published in the magazine *Nachnoe Obozrenie* (Scientific Review). This astonishing paper discussed the use of rockets powered by a mixture of liquid oxygen and hydrogen (the fuel used in the Space Shuttle) to explore space. That this was written before the first powered flight and by a completely self-educated man makes it even more surprising, and Tsiolkovsky went on to write about space trains, multi-stage rockets, and the need for pressurized suits for spacecraft occupants. Although his work remained almost completely theoretical, it provided the foundation for much that followed, and it's not surprising that Tsiolkovsky is regarded as the father of cosmonautics in Russia. Tsiolkovsky survived the Russian Revolution and continued to work in the Soviet Union until his death in 1935. He bequeathed the results of his life's work to the state, and this became the theoretical underpinning for much of the Russian space program.

Tsiolkovsky's American counterpart took a much more practical approach to the possibility of space flight. Robert H. Goddard was born in 1882 and became both a physicist and a professor, but he was also a prolific inventor and an engineer who registered more than 200 patents in the United States. Like Tsiolkovsky, Goddard first became interested in the possibility of space flight after reading science fiction, though in his case it was *The War of the Worlds* by H. G. Wells which he read soon after it was published in 1897.

Goddard gained a degree in physics from Worcester Polytechnic Institute (a private research university in Massachusetts) in 1904 and, following recovery from a near-fatal bout of tuberculosis, he became an instructor and research fellow at Clark University, another private research university in Massachusetts in 1914. There, he began to build and launch rockets. In the years that followed, Goddard and his team launched a number of solid fuel rockets that reached altitudes of almost two miles and speeds of over five hundred miles per hour.

In 1919, Goddard published *A Method of Reaching Extreme Altitudes*, which became one of the standard texts for U.S. space research. Ironically, given that both Goddard and Tsiolkovsky had been inspired by science fiction, in the first half of the twentieth century most people regarded rocketry as something from the realm of fantasy. A large number of established scientists claimed that Goddard's theories were mistaken and that using rockets to propel a spacecraft outside the Earth's atmosphere was impossible. In an article in the *New York Times* in 1920, Goddard and his theories were so violently ridiculed that he became extremely secretive and did not publicly discuss the results of most of his subsequent experiments.

In terms of public perception, the notion of rockets became indelibly linked not with real science, but with the fantasy of the Buck Rogers and Flash Gordon comic strips. This ridicule of rocketry became so intense that respectable scientists avoided using the "R-word" wherever possible, even when they were involved in rocket research. For example, when in 1936 the respected Guggenheim Aeronautical Laboratory at the California Institute of Technology (GALCIT) decided to form a group to study the practical applications of rockets, it was called the Jet Propulsion Laboratory (JPL), even though jets were never produced or studied there. When the JPL began to produce rocket pods in 1941 to be used on American military aircraft to allow them to take-off in short distances, these were called Jet-Assisted Take-Off (JATO) units, even though they were not jets. Jets, it seemed, were safely scientific while rockets were still regarded as silly.

It took the Nazis to make people think seriously about rockets. There was nothing remotely whimsical about V2 rockets, the world's first ballistic missiles which used the kind of liquid-fuel engines first imagined by Tsiolkovsky to carry more than 2,000 pounds of high explosive over 50 miles above the Earth at speeds of over 3,000 miles per hour. Thousands of people were killed by these deadly Nazi weapons during World War II, and suddenly rocketry was no longer the amusing province of science fiction.

Robert Goddard died in August 1945, just as World War II was ending and as public and scientific perception of his life's work was beginning to change.

Chapter Two

From Missiles to Rockets

"Don't tell me that Man doesn't belong out there. Man belongs wherever he wants to go—and he'll do plenty well when he gets there."

—Wernher von Braun

The rocket wasn't the only new technology developed during World War II. The United States also produced the first nuclear weapons. It didn't take long for military minds to start wondering about the possibility of combining these two new inventions to create rockets that could deliver nuclear weapons. And with the Nazis and the Japanese defeated, America began to realize that it faced a new and perhaps even more dangerous rival: the Soviet Union.

Almost before World War II was over, the two new superpowers began to maneuver for position in Europe. The countries of Eastern Europe became part of the Warsaw Pact, a military alliance dominated by the Soviet Union. Countries in the west of Europe joined the North Atlantic Treaty Organization (NATO), another military alliance, but this time dominated by America.

By 1949, the Soviet Union also had nuclear weapons. Initially, nuclear bombs were designed to be carried by aircraft, but these were too easy to intercept. What was needed was a way of delivering a nuclear weapon into the territory of the enemy as quickly and reliably as possible. Suddenly, the possession of rocket technology to deliver nuclear warheads became of extreme importance in both the United States and the Soviet Union.

At the close of the war in Europe, America had set out to find as many Nazi designers and technicians as possible in the hope of persuading these men to move to the U.S. to continue their research. Operation Paperclip brought over 1,600 Nazi scientists to America. Amongst these were almost all of the team behind the design of the V2 rockets, including the lead designer, Dr. Wernher von Braun. Within a very short time, the American military began Project Hermes, where designers and technicians from the General Electric Corporation studied captured V2 rockets and worked with German scientists to produce American versions.

In April 1946, almost one year after the end of the war, the first captured V2 was launched at the White Sands Proving Ground in New Mexico. Almost immediately, Wernher von Braun and his German colleagues began improving the basic V2 design. Within a few years, the missiles being launched from New Mexico were virtually unrecognizable as V2s—later versions were almost 50 percent heavier than the original, and many had small wings and control surfaces which helped maintain control.

By 1948, von Braun and his team of scientists were allowed to apply for American citizenship and became an important part of the missile program. In 1950, von Braun relocated to the Redstone Arsenal near Huntsville in Alabama where he began work on the Redstone, a ballistic missile intended for the U.S. Army. Von Braun was fascinated by the possibility of space travel, however, and he began lobbying to have funds diverted from the design of missiles to the design of passenger-carrying rockets which could be used for the exploration of space.

At the time, there was little interest in space travel, and the American administration believed that it was necessary to focus all their efforts into the production of ever more powerful Intercontinental Ballistic Missiles (ICBMs) capable of delivering nuclear warheads into the Russian heartlands. Von Braun continued development of the Redstone rocket which was capable of carrying a nuclear warhead to an altitude of over 25 miles. He was aware, however, that the rockets his team designed for the U.S. Army were also capable of carrying a smaller payload outside the Earth's atmosphere.

In Russia, aircraft designer Sergei Pavlovich Korolev was given the task of examining German rockets after World War II and developing Soviet versions of these missiles. Korolev had been the president of a small amateur rocket club before the war, and he had helped design rocket packs for Russian military aircraft. As soon as the war ended, he was inducted into the Russian army and sent to Germany to collect as many V2 rockets and parts as possible and to identify captured German scientists who might be persuaded to join the Russian missile development team. In doing this, he was competing with the Americans who were doing precisely the same thing. The space race was preceded by a race to gain access to as much German missile research information and technology as possible.

Korolev was able to find a number of German engineers and technicians who had been involved in the V2 program (though not the senior designers, who had mostly gone to America), and a Special Design Bureau, OKB-1, was established 200 miles from Moscow where work began on producing a Russian copy of the V2. This missile, designated the R-1, was first launched in October 1947. Just like the Americans, the Russians rapidly improved the V2 design with the R-2 and R-3 rockets. The latter—launched for the first time in 1949—had a range of 2,000 miles, 10 times the range of the original V2. In the early 1950s, Korolev and his team began work on the R-7, the world's first true ICBM. The R-7 was a two-stage rocket comprising a central core with four liquid fuel boosters attached. It was capable of carrying a payload of five tons to a range of four and a half thousand miles.

Unlike von Braun and his team, Korolev's name was virtually unknown within the USSR, and his identity was a complete mystery to those in the West. To most of his team, he was known only by the initials SP (for Sergei Pavlovich) or, more commonly, just as the "Chief Designer." But just like von Braun in America, Korolev was fascinated by the possibility of exploring space, and he knew that the R-7 was also capable of carrying a small payload into space. In May 1954, he sent a secret document, *Report on an artificial Satellite of the Earth*, to the Soviet government. This report pointed out that American scientists were already interested in space and recommended using the R-7 to launch a small satellite into Earth's orbit.

In February 1955, a panel of experts in the U.S. government Technological Capabilities Panel issued a secret report, *Meeting the Threat of Surprise Attack*. This discussed the importance of space in a military context and the use of reconnaissance satellites to monitor the Soviet Union. It recommended the launch of a satellite into Earth's orbit as quickly as possible.

Gradually, the administrations in America and the Soviet Union came to see the strategic advantages of being able to place objects in Earth's orbit. Initially, these were seen as most likely being reconnaissance units or weapon guidance systems, but later the possibility of placing people in space was also considered. Holding the high ground has always been recognized as a military advantage, and space provides the ultimate high ground. Both in America and in Russia, it was recognized that the country that reached space first would have a decisive military advantage. By the mid-1950s, both sides had come to recognize that reaching space as quickly as possible was a military necessity.

In May 1955, the U.S. National Security Council (NSC) reviewed plans for the launch of a satellite. It agreed that being the first nation to launch such a satellite would bring great prestige and would establish the principle of the "freedom of space"—that a country's sovereign territory did not extend beyond the Earth's atmosphere. On July 29, 1955, James Hagerty, President Eisenhower's press secretary, held a press conference at which he announced that the United States would launch a "science satellite" into Earth's orbit before the end of the International Geophysical Year, which would last from July 1957 to December 1958. Just four days later, on August 2, the Soviet Union responded with a press conference at the International Astronautical Congress in Copenhagen, Denmark at which they announced that "the realization of the Soviet satellite project can be expected in the near future."

With these announcements, the space race had begun.

Chapter Three

Russia Takes the Lead

"Some say God is living there [in space]. I was looking around very attentively, but I did not see anyone there. I did not detect either angels or gods. . . . I don't believe in God. I believe in man—his strength, his possibilities, his reason."

—Gherman Titov

In the United States, the space program was originally controlled by the National Advisory Committee for Aeronautics (NACA), a body formed during World War I to examine and evaluate new technology related to military aviation. NACA was closely tied to the U.S. Air Force and in the mid-1950s was already involved in research on subjects relating to missiles and supersonic flight. This included research on the re-entry of spacecraft, which was intended to be applied to nuclear missiles traveling outside the Earth's atmosphere, but it was also clearly relevant to manned space flight.

Once it became clear that the administration of President Eisenhower was prepared to support the development of space vehicles, NACA began to look at much more ambitious plans, including the launch of manned spacecraft. Although President Eisenhower was supportive of efforts to put an American satellite in orbit, he was concerned that this might be construed as a warlike act, especially given that the orbit of the satellite would inevitably bring it above territory controlled by the Soviet Union.

The most advanced rocket in the United States at the time was the Jupiter-C, designed by von Braun and his team for the U.S. Army. The Jupiter-C was purely a military project intended to carry a nuclear missile. Rather than use a Jupiter-C for the first satellite launch, Eisenhower insisted that the Vanguard rocket designed by the Naval Research Laboratory be used instead. The Vanguard design wasn't as advanced as that of the Jupiter-C, but although commissioned by the U.S. Navy it had been not been primarily designed as a military rocket— the Vanguard was a scientific research rocket which was not capable of carrying a substantial warhead. So, it was decided that the U.S. Navy would be responsible for preparing the Vanguard as the platform for the launch of the first American satellite.

At that time, there was an assumption that the United States was far in advance of the Soviet Union in terms of missile development, so there wasn't any real concern that the Russians might get there first. But in Russia, Korolev and his design team were watching developments in America carefully. When on September 20, 1956, von Braun's team launched the first test of the Jupiter-C rocket, the Russians assumed that this had been a failed attempt to launch a satellite. It wasn't—the test was a successful suborbital evaluation of the warhead re-entry design. However, this spurred the Russian Design Bureau to accelerate its satellite launch plans.

Originally, the intention had been to use the powerful R-7 rocket to launch a massive satellite weighing over 3,000 pounds which would carry cameras and equipment for taking readings of radiation levels. Design of this satellite was taking more time than anticipated so, in order to be able to launch more quickly, a much smaller and simpler satellite, Prosteishy Sputnik 1 (PS-1), was created. Sputnik 1 would be a sphere just 58 cm in diameter and weighing less than 200 pounds. Instead of complex instrumentation, Sputnik 1 contained only two short-wave radio transmitters operating on different frequencies and each set to broadcast a series of beeps. In terms of scientific investigation, Sputnik 1 was almost completely pointless. But in terms of prestige, the first country to successfully launch a satellite of any kind would gain a great deal.

In September 1957, another Jupiter-C rocket was launched. Once again, this had nothing to do with American efforts to put a satellite into orbit, but again Korolev's team interpreted this as the final test before a satellite launch. Then it became know that American scientists were to present a paper at the National Academy of Sciences in Washington DC on October 6. The paper was titled "Satellite Over the Planet." The Russians became convinced that the Americans intended to launch a satellite to coincide with the presentation of this paper. They were mistaken—the Vanguard rocket was not even close to being ready for launch, and the paper was merely intended as a report on progress to date. But to ensure that Russia got there first, Korolev scheduled the launch of Sputnik 1 for October 4, 1957.

The launch was to take place at the newly named Baikonur Cosmodrome, a missile launch facility in southern Kazakhstan. Sputnik 1 was mounted on a modified R-7 rocket and, at 10:28 pm Moscow time, the launch took place. For a very nervous 95 minutes, personnel at the launch site waited. Then, their radio receivers finally picked up the distinctive "beep, beep, beep" of Sputnik 1 as it passed over Baikonur having completed its first orbit. The first human-made satellite was successfully orbiting the Earth.

The reaction in the Soviet Union was euphoric. There was a general perception that America was more technologically advanced than Russia, but the launch of Sputnik 1 seemed to show that the opposite was true. On October 5, Pravda proudly reported: "Artificial satellites of the Earth will pave the way to interplanetary travel and, possibly, our contemporaries are destined to witness how the freed and meaningful labor of the people of the new socialist society makes a reality the most daring dreams of humanity."

In America, the reaction was one of extreme dismay. Was this new satellite a weapon? How could the Soviet Union possibly have beaten the industrial and technological might of the United States? The *New York Herald Tribune* printed an open letter from economist Bernard Baruch titled "The Lessons of Defeat." The letter noted: "It is Russia, not the United States, who has had the imagination to hitch its wagon to the stars and the skill to reach for the moon and all but grasp it. America is worried. It should be." On October 9, science fiction writer Arthur C. Clarke announced that "the day Sputnik orbited around the Earth, the United States became a second-rate power." The Democrats attacked the Eisenhower administration for allowing the Soviet Union to gain such a decisive advantage in the space race.

Five days after the launch of Sputnik 1, President Eisenhower addressed the American people. He reassured them by acknowledging that while the launch of a satellite was a notable scientific advance, analysis showed that Sputnik 1 had no military capability. He also implied that the United States would soon equal or surpass the Soviet achievement. Privately, he insisted that the launch of a satellite on a Vanguard rocket should be brought forward and should take place as soon as possible.

Meanwhile, the Russian premier, Nikita Khrushchev, instructed Korolev to launch a second satellite into orbit to coincide with the 40th anniversary of the Bolshevik Revolution. On November 3, 1957, just 32 days after the launch of Sputnik 1, Russia successfully launched Sputnik 2, and this time, the satellite contained a living space traveler—a dog named Laika. The unfortunate canine died a few hours after launch, but it seemed to most Americans that the Soviet Union was able to launch space vehicles at will while the United States had failed to put a single item in orbit.

Russia appeared to have taken a decisive lead in the space race, and the Eisenhower administration decided to

respond directly and in the most public way possible—
with their own successful satellite launch.

Chapter Four

Early American Failures

"Will outer space be preserved for peaceful use and developed for the benefit of all mankind? Or will it become another focus for the arms race--and thus an area of dangerous and sterile competition? The choice is urgent. And it is ours to make."

—Dwight D. Eisenhower

The American response to the Soviet Sputnik launches was the two-stage U.S. Navy Vanguard rocket, built by the Martin Company and designed by the Naval Research Laboratory (NRL). Compared to the Russian R-7, the Vanguard had very limited capacity and power; it was designed specifically as a rocket used for delivering science monitoring equipment to space, not carrying a heavy nuclear warhead.

When American scientists working on the Vanguard project first heard that Sputnik 1 weighed two hundred pounds, they were convinced the Soviets must be exaggerating. They had no way of knowing that the Russian rocket was much more powerful than the American version and was capable of lifting ten times as much at over two thousand pounds of payload. In contrast, the first American satellite weighed just under three pounds, near to the maximum payload the Vanguard was capable of lifting. At just over six inches in diameter, the U.S. TV-3 satellite was truly tiny—Russian premier Nikita Khrushchev referred to it derisively as "the grapefruit." But the size of the satellite was irrelevant—provided that they could successfully launch anything at all into Earth's orbit, America could reasonably claim to have caught up with the Russians.

The U.S. Navy team behind the Vanguard project was under intense pressure to accomplish the launch of a satellite before the end of 1957. They pushed ahead with final preparations, and by mid-November the rocket was placed at the Cape Canaveral rocket launch site on a spit of land off the coast of Florida.

The launch was set for December 4, 1957. Thousands of people gathered on roads and beaches to watch the historic launch of America's first satellite. However, during final checks, a liquid oxygen valve was found to have frozen and, at just after ten o'clock that evening, the launch was cancelled. After feverish activity by technicians, the problem was fixed, and a new launch date was announced—December 6. Launch preparation started at 01:00 and the launch countdown began at 17:00. Once again, large numbers of people gathered to watch. A number of minor issues were identified during the countdown and subsequently fixed. The launch gantry was removed, and final preparations were made for launch. Finally, it seemed, America was ready to enter the space age.

At 11:44 Eastern Time, a young Navy engineer, Paul Karpiscak, pressed the launch button. The Vanguard's main engines ignited with a mighty roar, and the rocket soared off the launch pad. Well, perhaps "soared" isn't the right word because the Vanguard rocket managed to lift itself just four feet off the ground before it became apparent that something was very wrong. The rocket seemed to falter and hang just above the launch pad for a moment before it sank back to the ground and exploded in a huge fireball. In the most public way possible, it had become apparent that America wasn't just losing the space race, it hadn't yet managed to leave the starting blocks.

The cause of the failure was never established, but it was assumed to have been caused by a fuel leak or a faulty fuel line. It didn't really matter—the embarrassment was total. American newspapers had a field day inventing puns from the word "sputnik" to describe the Vanguard fiasco. "Stayputnik," "Oopsnik," "Kaputnik," and "Flopnik" were just a few of the favorites. Trading in the Martin Company—the manufacturers of the rocket—had to be suspended on the U.S. Stock Exchange when sell orders on the company's stock reached epidemic proportions following the disaster. Bars around the United States began offering so-called Sputnik Cocktails—one-third vodka and two-thirds sour grapes. A Russian delegate to the United Nations enquired whether America was interested in receiving help from the Soviet Union; Russia offered a program of technical assistance to backward nations, he happily explained.

The Vanguard program had a backup rocket, but the launch site had been badly damaged by the explosion. Repairs were finally completed in early January 1958, and a new Vanguard rocket was placed on the launch gantry. Torrential rain caused major problems, however, including the shorting of essential electrical connections. There were three attempts to launch the satellite during January, but all had to be called off due to technical problems. It was clear the U.S. Navy program was not going to provide an American satellite in the near future.

In Alabama, the U.S. Army team led by von Braun had been preparing for just such a failure. They had been disappointed when their Jupiter-C rocket hadn't been chosen to launch the first American satellite, but they had gone ahead with preparations of a small satellite, Explorer 1. The Army's Jupiter-C rocket was moved to a launch pad at Cape Canaveral in early January 1958, and a launch date of January 29 was agreed. It was assumed that this would follow the launch of one of the remaining Vanguard rockets, but with continuing delays to the Vanguard launch, it began to look as though von Braun's team might be the first to launch an American satellite into orbit. The Eisenhower administration was now so desperate to negate the embarrassment of the Vanguard failure that it was willing to use a military rocket if this would allow them to catch up to the Russians.

General Medaris, the Army commander with responsibility for the Jupiter-C program, deliberately kept details of the planned launch secret—there was no advance publicity about the launch until January 28.

Unfortunately, bad weather on January 29 meant that the launch was postponed. Final countdown for the launch didn't begin until 13:30 on January 31. At 21:45 there was a short hold when a hydrogen peroxide leak was noticed. This was rectified, and the countdown restarted after a 15-minute delay. With 12 seconds remaining, the motors were started and at 22:48, the Jupiter-C rocket lifted off without a hitch and, 440 seconds later, the second stage engine fired on schedule. The rocket continued to accelerate into the night sky as the third and fourth stage engines fired.

At 12:51 on February 1, 1958, one hour and fifty-three minutes after take-off, a tracking station in California was the first to pick up a transmission from the satellite. Explorer 1 was orbiting the Earth, and America had finally entered the space age. The reaction in the United States was very positive; Wernher von Braun and members of the Jupiter-C team were pictured at a press conference triumphantly holding a model of the rocket aloft. Explorer 1 continued to broadcast a radio signal for just 31 days before its batteries died, but it had achieved its purpose.

Despite the euphoria over the successful launch of Explorer 1, problems with U.S. launch vehicles weren't completely solved. When a second Vanguard rocket was launched on February 5, 1957, it managed to get off the launch gantry, but it exploded at an altitude of just 1,500 feet. On March 5, the Army launched a second Jupiter-C rocket carrying Explorer 2. However, the fourth stage of the rocket failed to fire, and the satellite plummeted into the Atlantic Ocean and was lost. This unreliability was a major concern given that the next stage of the space race would involve sending humans into orbit.

Chapter Five

The First Men in Space

"I see Earth. It is so beautiful!"

—Yuri Gagarin, first words in space

One of the results of the successful American satellite launch was extended discussion about which agency should take control of the U.S. space program. The inter-service rivalry between the Navy Vanguard and the Army Jupiter-C was unhelpful and wasteful. In the end, it was decided that control of the space program should be handled by a special civilian body set up outside the Department of Defense, and on October 1, 1958, the National Aeronautics and Space Administration (NASA) was formed with Thomas Keith Glennan, president of the Case Institute of Technology in Cleveland, as its first administrator.

In Russia, Sergei Korolev and his team of engineers began to work towards the next logical step in the space race—manned space flight. The Soviet space program was still dependent on funds from the military, so Korolev was charged with designing a launch vehicle that could be used to launch both large reconnaissance satellites and some form of manned space vehicle. In the late 1950s, he began work on the Vostok (East) spacecraft. The first version, the Vostok-L, was similar to the R-7 rocket though it used more powerful engines. It was tested during 1959, and the first test launch took place on May 15, 1960. For the first test, the rocket carried the Korabl-Sputnik (Starship Satellite). This was an unmanned vehicle, though it was used to test many of the functions of the planned manned craft.

The Korabl-Sputnik (later re-named the Vostok Spacecraft) comprised a cylindrical body containing engines and instruments and a descent module in which there was room for a single cosmonaut. Space inside the 2.3-meter diameter module was very tight indeed, and one of the essential prerequisites for any early Soviet cosmonaut was that they could not be more than five feet, four inches tall. The descent module was designed to separate from the main body and then deploy parachutes when it entered the atmosphere. The cosmonaut was required to eject from the capsule at an altitude of around 20,000 feet and descend separately. Lessons learned from early tests resulted in the production of the Vostok 3KA Spacecraft, an improved version of the Korabl-Sputnik with limited thruster ability and room for a single cosmonaut.

In America, Project Mercury was initiated in October 1958 under the control of the newly formed NASA and with the objective of placing a manned spacecraft in orbit around the Earth. The design of the Mercury spacecraft differed from the Russian Vostok—the Mercury capsule was bigger with more internal space (a pilot of up to five feet and eleven inches in height could be accommodated), and it was conical in shape with a heat-shield at the broad end. When the capsule entered the Earth's atmosphere, parachutes were deployed, and all Mercury missions were planned to allow the capsule to splash-down in an ocean with the astronaut still inside. The Jupiter-C rocket used for the early satellite launches was not suitable for the heavier Mercury craft, so a new launch vehicle, the Atlas-D rocket was produced by modifying the existing Atlas ICBM.

In both Russia and America there was a concerted effort to recruit cosmonauts and astronauts. In general and in both countries, the search was amongst pilots with military experience. There was no shortage of volunteers in either country, but in Russia the selection process was narrowed by the lack of space in the Vostok capsule. The selection process for potential space crew was extremely stringent—no one knew what physical challenges space travel might involve, so only men with exceptional strength and stamina were selected.

In America, the selection process produced seven potential astronauts. These men, the "Mercury Seven" were introduced to the American public on April 9, 1959. Three were Air Force pilots, three were Navy pilots, and one was a pilot from the Marine Corps. These seven men became national heroes in the United States, and all were featured in television and newspaper interviews. After being beaten by the Soviet Union in the launching of the first satellite, most Americans were confident that one of these seven men would be the first man in space.

In Russia, the selection of potential cosmonauts proceeded in complete secrecy. By the end of 1959, twenty Red Air Force pilots had been selected for cosmonaut training and sent to Star City, a training center in Moscow Oblast. All twenty went through advanced training, and by January 1961, this group was reduced to just six men who were considered to have the physical and mental capabilities to become cosmonauts.

In America, astronaut training was undertaken at a number of U.S. Air Force and Navy establishments, and the seven potential astronauts were also involved in the final design refinements of the Mercury capsule. The Mercury schedule envisaged a first manned sub-orbital flight before sending a man into Earth's orbit. A number of test launches of unmanned Mercury capsules and mock-ups were undertaken in late 1960 and early 1961. These were generally successful, and test flights were also undertaken with chimpanzees in the Mercury capsule. These were a success, and a manned sub-orbital flight was planned for May 1961.

The Americans had little information about the progress of the Soviet program, and it was confidently assumed that an American would be the first man in space. Then, on April 12, 1961, there came a shattering surprise—newspapers and television news reports around the world were filled with photographs of a grinning Russian Air Force pilot. Yuri Gagarin had completed a successful orbital flight after the launch of Vostok 1 from Baikonur Cosmodrome.

After a single orbit of the Earth, Gagarin had made a safe landing in the Saratov region of Russia. The petite Gagarin (he was just five feet and two inches tall) became a national hero in Russia and an international celebrity. In America, there was once again dismay. Somehow, the Russians had beaten them once again. When, three weeks later, Alan Shepard became the first American in space when he undertook a short sub-orbital hop in a Mercury spacecraft, it felt like a consolation prize. It took almost one year before John Glenn equaled Gagarin's flight and made a single orbit of the Earth in February 1962.

Somehow, Russia kept beating the United States to important space milestones. But the next goal for the space race was to be most complex and challenging yet, and this time, America was determined to be there first.

Chapter Six

The Race to the Moon

"We choose to go to the moon in this decade and do the other things, not because they are easy, but because they are hard."

—John F. Kennedy

By November 1960, a new president of the United States had been elected—Democrat John F. Kennedy. During the elections, Kennedy had repeatedly attacked the Eisenhower administration for allowing the Russians to gain a lead in important military hardware. The term "the missile gap" was coined during the election to describe a perceived imbalance between the number of American nuclear missiles and the number of missiles fielded by the Russians. The truth was that no such gap existed—this misapprehension was based on faulty intelligence. However, there were close ties between the Soviet space program and their ability to produce nuclear missiles. For many Americans, the Russian lead in space strongly suggested that they were also leading in the production of secret missile technology.

But when Kennedy was formally sworn-in as president in January 1961, his support for the U.S. space program was not particularly strong. When the NASA administrator presented a proposal to Kennedy in March 1961 for a program which would lead to a manned moon landing by 1970, the president rejected it out of hand. It was, he said, simply too expensive. Then in April came Yuri Gagarin's flight. Kennedy became aware of just how frightening and threatening most Americans found the apparent Russian lead in the space race, and he asked his vice-president, Lyndon B. Johnson, to assess what would be needed to allow America to take the lead. Johnson reported that the next significant milestone in the space race would be a manned landing on the moon. It would take a number of years to achieve this, but—if sufficient funds were allocated—it seemed reasonable to expect that America could beat the Russians to the moon.

On May 25, 1961, President Kennedy asked Congress for funding for the U.S. moon landing program in a speech titled "Special Message on Urgent National Needs." In this, he suggested that America "should commit itself to achieving the goal, before this decade is out, of landing a man on the moon and returning him safely to the Earth."

It was a bold move. Thus far, America had lagged behind in the exploration of space. The president was committing his country to completing an incredibly difficult and dangerous task within less than ten years. Some Americans were happy that their country finally seemed to be taking the race into space seriously. Others were concerned, both at the huge costs of such a program and at whether America actually had the expertise and technology to achieve this goal. Ex-President Eisenhower said, "To spend $40 billion to reach the moon is just nuts!"

In September 1961, Kennedy followed up his speech to Congress with a public address in which spoke about the space race. On September 12, the president addressed a crowd of around 40,000 people in the Rice University football stadium in Texas. He likened space to the frontiers of the old West in America and evoked the pioneering spirit of the first explorers there. He spoke about space itself, often in a romantic and appealing way, and about America's role in its exploration: "We set sail on this new sea because there is new knowledge to be gained and new rights to be won and they must be won for the progress of all people. Only if the United States occupies a position of pre-eminence can we help decide whether this new ocean will be a sea of peace or a new, terrifying theatre of war."

Kennedy went on to talk about the difficulties and dangers involved, and in the most memorable and often quoted part of his speech he said: "We choose to go to the moon! We choose to go to the moon in this decade and do the other things, not because they are easy, but because they are hard; because that goal will serve to organize and measure the best of our energies and skills, because that challenge is one that we are willing to accept, one we are unwilling to postpone, and one we intend to win."

More than any other single event, this speech helped to stir great interest in space exploration, both in the United States and elsewhere. It also publicly committed America not only to facing and overcoming the technical challenges of landing a man on the moon but of doing so within ten years and before anyone else. For many Americans, it became unpatriotic not to support the moon landing program, despite its huge cost. The next phase of the space race would be the most demanding and difficult yet, and if America could not deliver on the ambition and hope in President Kennedy's speeches, Russia would truly have won the race into space.

Uncharacteristically, the Russian leader, Nikita Khrushchev, did not respond to the challenge to the Soviet Union inherent in Kennedy's speech. Part of the issue was that Russia had no equivalent of NASA, no centralized body responsible for the kind of long-term planning and focused effort needed to place a man on the moon. Soviet space development was in the hands of a number of separate design bureaus, often working for different ministries and competing against one another for scarce funding and resources. The relatively short-term goals of placing a satellite in orbit and putting a man into space were achievable using the offshoots of the ICBM program available to Korolev and his team. Placing a man on the moon would require a long-term effort and could not afford the kind of internal squabbling which characterized many Soviet design projects.

As early as 1959, Korolev appealed directly to Khrushchev, asking him to form a single centralized body to oversee the Soviet space program, but this was refused. Instead, Korolev was expected to personally oversee and control all projects related to space in the Soviet Union.

The Vostok program continued with five more manned missions which claimed many other firsts for Russia. In August 1962, Vostok 2 allowed a cosmonaut to spend a full day in space, Vostok 3 and 4 were launched simultaneously, Vostok 5 performed the longest orbital flight to date on June 14, 1963, and two days later Vostok 6 made Valentina Tereshkova the first woman in space. The interest and kudos attached to the development of space vehicles attracted the interest of other design bureaus in Russia, and by the time of the last Vostok launch, there were at least four agencies competing for contracts.

After Vostok, Sergei Korolev and OKB-1 had hoped to begin work on a completely new spacecraft, one capable of reaching the moon. Instead, Korolev was told to concentrate on near-Earth missions and to create an updated version of Vostok instead. This became the Voskhod program, with a larger, more powerful version of the Vostok rocket. There were just two manned Voskhod flights, one in 1964 and one in 1965. Both were deliberately undertaken to beat the Americans to some new space milestone—Voskhod 1 was the first multi-crew vehicle in space, and the crew of Voskhod 2 performed the first spacewalk.

Nikita Khrushchev was removed from power in October 1964 and replaced by a new Russian leader, Leonid Brezhnev. Brezhnev was much less interested in the kind of stunts that had pleased Khrushchev, and the Soviet space program was able to settle into a new pattern, following the dictates of science and developing technology rather than focusing on beating the Americans. It was now obvious that Russia needed a completely new spacecraft if it was to have any hope of competing with the United States in a race to put a man on the moon. It was equally obvious that the other agencies competing with OKB-1 which had been given responsibility for this massive and complex project were making very little progress.

Chapter Seven

Fatalities on Both Sides

"Many years ago the great British explorer George Mallory, who was to die on Mount Everest, was asked why did he want to climb it. He said 'Because it is there.' Well, space is there, and we're going to climb it, and the moon and the planets are there, and new hopes for knowledge and peace are there."

—John F. Kennedy

In America, the Mercury program continued with a total of six manned flights culminating in an orbital flight lasting more than one day on May 15, 1963. Even before the final Mercury launch, work was progressing on the next generation of U.S. space hardware—Project Gemini. The Gemini capsule was bigger, providing room for a two-man crew and launched on a more powerful rocket. Unlike the Soviet program, the Gemini was always intended as a research vehicle which would provide information that could be used to design a spacecraft capable of reaching the moon, and there was no pressure on members of this project to achieve the kind of firsts which came to dominate the work of their Russian counterparts.

In 1965 and 1966, Gemini crews flew ten low orbit missions during which they performed spacewalks, rendezvoused two Gemini spacecraft, and spent up to 14 days in space, proving that the endurance needed for a moon mission was possible. The final Gemini flight took place in November 1966 when one of the crew, Edwin "Buzz" Aldrin, performed a spacewalk that lasted over five hours. The Gemini program was entirely successful and provided vital experience and training for the astronauts who would be involved in the moon mission.

The design of the moon mission hardware, Project Apollo, was already well advanced while the Gemini missions were taking place. The design called for a specialized heavy launch vehicle, the Saturn rocket, which would launch a command module (incorporating a three-man crew capsule) attached to a two-stage lunar lander. The command module would orbit the moon while the lander descended. After the landing, the upper section of the lander would blast off and re-join the command module. Then, the lander would be discarded, and the command module would return to Earth.

Many of the Gemini missions were specifically designed to test aspects of the Apollo mission profile—for example, testing the ability to reliably rendezvous in space was an essential part of the Gemini program. The project proceeded in measured steps towards the final goal of placing a man on the moon and bringing him safely back to Earth. There was no pressure to beat the Russians to any short-term goals (though most Americans hoped this would be possible), but when in November 1963 President

John F. Kennedy was assassinated, to a certain extent, Apollo became his memorial. Inside the project, there was a growing determination to achieve the first moon landing within the timespan the president had forecasted, before the end of 1969.

Meanwhile, in October 1965, development started in Russia of the Giant N-1 rocket, a super-heavy lift launch vehicle which was intended to be used to take a man to the moon, as well as a smaller Soyuz rocket. In January 1966, the Soviet space program suffered a massive setback, however, when Sergei Korolev died following what should have been a routine operation. He was replaced in his role as head of OKB-1 by Vasily Mishin, a talented engineer, but a man who was notably less able at navigating the labyrinthine corridors of power in the Soviet Union. Mishin took over the Soyuz program and was given the task of sending a cosmonaut around the moon in 1967 and performing a moon landing by 1968 using the N-1. In both cases, he was naturally expected to beat the Americans.

In the United States, the first manned test flight of the Apollo spacecraft was scheduled for February 21, 1967. The flight was to be a low orbit test of the command module. On January 27, testing was in progress, and the men who were intended to be the three first Apollo astronauts—Virgil "Gus" Grissom, Ed White, and Roger B. Chaffee—were strapped into their seats in the cramped capsule. Suddenly, a fire broke out inside the capsule. All three men died before they could be extricated. These were the first fatalities directly associated with the U.S. space program, and everyone involved was stunned.

Following the tragedy, a number of new safety features were added to the Apollo spacecraft. The next Apollo launches were all unmanned tests. These were successful, and the next manned mission, Apollo 7, was scheduled for October 1968. The Apollo schedule had suddenly become very tight if a man was to walk on the moon before the end of the decade, but the scientists and designers involved were confident that the project was still achievable.

Just three months after the fire which killed the American astronauts, Russia launched Soyuz 1, the first test of this new spacecraft and the first launch under the control of Vasily Mishin. The mission was plagued with difficulties from the start; it had been planned to rendezvous with Soyuz 2, but the second spacecraft was unable to take off due to bad weather. There were a number of electrical problems with the craft, and during its final descent the main parachutes failed; the sole member of the crew, Vladimir Komarov, died when the descent module smashed into the ground at Orenburg Oblast. A subsequent investigation found a number of problems with the Soyuz craft, and the next launch would not take place until 18 months later, in October 1968.

Work on the giant N-1 rocket was not going well—it was becoming apparent that the design and development of this rocket had been rushed, causing major technical problems. These delays meant that it would not be possible for Mishin to meet his targets for a Russian moon mission. Mishin was also widely criticized within the Russian space program for his inability to make progress and for his increasing reliance on alcohol. Almost for the first time, the Russians seemed to be falling behind the Americans in the space race.

The Apollo program was increasing in tempo. On October 11, 1968, Apollo 7 launched to complete the first manned orbital mission. Just two months later, Apollo 8 achieved the first manned trip to the moon and completed ten orbits before returning safely to Earth. In March 1969, Apollo 9 achieved the first deployment of the command and lunar modules, though this was done in Earth's orbit. In May 1969, Apollo 10 carried out a successful rehearsal for a manned moon landing mission, descending to within 50,000 feet of the lunar surface. NASA announced that the next Apollo mission would take a man to the surface of the moon.

Russia responded with the first unmanned attempt to launch the giant N-1 rocket in February 1969. The rocket failed to leave the launch pad due to a number of technical issues. On July 3, 1969, in a desperate attempt to draw attention away from American progress with the Apollo missions, a second attempt was made to launch an unmanned N-1, this time on a mission to orbit the moon. This launch proved to be record-breaking, but not in the way that Mishin and his team had hoped. The N-1 cleared the launch gantry but then exploded. The detonation was the most powerful non-nuclear explosion in human history. When launch crews emerged from their bunkers

30 minutes after the explosion, fragments of debris and unburned fuel were still drifting to Earth.

With the destruction of the second N-1 rocket, any realistic hope of the Soviet Union competing with the United States for the first moon landing ended. All the Russians could now do was wait and watch the American moon landing attempt.

Chapter Eight

The Moon Landing

"One small step for a man, one giant leap for mankind."

—Neil Armstrong

On July 16, 1969, Apollo 11 lifted off from Launch Pad 39A at the Kennedy Space Centre. Thousands of spectators crowded roads and beaches in the area to watch the launch. Millions more watched on television. This was the culmination of the space race. The mission was intended to take two of the three crew, Neil Armstrong and Buzz Aldrin, to the lunar surface while Michael Collins remained above in lunar orbit in the command module. The huge Saturn V rocket propelled Apollo into orbit 100 miles above the Earth without any problems. After completing just over one full orbit, the third-stage engine pushed the spacecraft out of orbit and into a trans-lunar injection, a trajectory towards the moon.

The mission went smoothly until the lunar module *Eagle* was on the last part of its descent towards the surface of the moon. During the final moments of descent, the craft's computers began sounding alarms— the planned landing site was covered with large boulders. Neil Armstrong took over manual control and calmly steered the craft to a clear area for a safe landing. When it finally touched down, *Eagle* had less than 30 seconds of fuel remaining. At 20:18 UTC on July 20, 1969, mission control received a terse radio message: "Houston, Tranquility Base here. The Eagle has landed."

Six hours later, with millions of people all around the world watching on television, Neil Armstrong stepped out of the lunar module and down onto the surface of the moon. *Eagle* remained on the lunar surface for twenty hours, and during that period the two astronauts spent around two and a half hours walking on the moon. At 05:54 UTC on July 21, *Eagle* lifted off from the moon and rendezvoused with the command module in lunar orbit. On the moon's surface, the Apollo 11 astronauts left a plaque which read: "Here men from the planet Earth first set foot upon the moon. July, 1969, AD. We came in peace for all mankind."

Apollo 11 returned to Earth and splashed down safely in the Pacific Ocean at 16:50 UTC on July 24. The mission had lasted eight days and had been a complete success. Although no one realized it at the time, it also marked the end of the space race between Russia and the United States. There were five more Apollo moon landings, culminating in the landing of the lunar module from Apollo 17 in the Taurus-Littrow area of the moon in December 1972 (Apollo 13 suffered an explosion in an oxygen tank which prevented it from reaching the moon).

There were no Russian moon landings. There were two more attempts to launch the N-1 rocket, one in 1971 and one in 1972, but both were failures; one involved yet another massive explosion and left a huge crater in the steppe. The two remaining N-1 rockets were dismantled when the project was formally canceled in 1976. Vasily Mishin had already been replaced as head of the Russian space program by Valentin Glushko in 1974. Mishin's replacement was thought to be mainly due to the failure of the N-1 rocket and the Russian moon landing project. There were no further attempts at a Russian moon landing, and the focus of Russian efforts in space switched to Earth orbit projects using the Soyuz rocket.

In America, NASA confidently presented President Nixon with ambitious plans which included more moon landings, the building of large space stations, the creation of a manned base on the moon, and a manned landing on Mars by 1986. All were rejected. The moon landings had engendered a huge upswelling of national pride in America, but the cost was crippling. The moon missions had required almost four percent of the national budget for eight years. As President Nixon explained, this wasn't a sustainable level of expenditure for any country. He said, "Space expenditures must take their proper place within a rigorous system of national priorities." Many people in government wanted Nixon to cancel the space program entirely, but instead he provided a reduced level of funding to NASA to enable it to develop what became the Space Shuttle program. The three remaining planned lunar landings, Apollo 18, 19, and 20, were all canceled.

The Soviet Union placed the first space station, Salyut 1, in orbit in April 1971, but this achievement was marred when the crew of Soyuz 11, returning to Earth from the station, died when their spacecraft lost air pressure.

America responded with Skylab, an orbital workstation launched in 1974.

Back in 1972, U.S. President Nixon and Soviet leader Leonid Brezhnev had negotiated formal treaties which created a temporary improvement in relations between the two countries. This led in May 1974 to a joint Apollo-Soyuz mission. The mission used the last remaining Apollo spacecraft to dock in Earth's orbit with a Russian Soyuz craft. The mission had little practical application, but it was intended as a public demonstration that the era of competition in space was over and that the Soviet Union and the United States were no longer in competition.

The détente lasted until the American Space Shuttle program began to gather pace in the mid-1970s. The Soviet Union responded with its most expensive space project ever—the VKK Space Orbiter project, generally known as the Buran (Blizzard) program. It involved a re-usable spacecraft that looked similar to the Space Shuttle, though it was very different in design terms. However, the Buran made only one unmanned orbital flight in 1988. By that time, the Soviet Union itself was losing cohesion, and just three years later it collapsed completely.

Conclusion

A space race of sorts continues today, though now it involves commercial companies competing with each other in addition to national space programs. Still, there is currently nothing to compare with the competition between the Soviet Union and the United States for the exploration of space which lasted for 12 years, from the launch of the first Sputnik to the moon landing. From 1957 to 1969, every new milestone in space travel was bitterly and publicly contested between the two superpowers. The race into space became a visible manifestation of the Cold War between these countries.

Initially, the Soviet Union's advantage appeared to confirm the belief that Russia had advanced beyond the United States in technological capacity. We now know that this was an illusion and that Russia never did have such an advantage either in terms of space vehicles or nuclear weapons. What the Soviets did have was a dedicated and able chief designer in Sergei Korolev. This man was able to focus the work of the Russian space program to make the best use of the resources that Russia possessed. In the early days of the space race, this gave the Soviets a distinct advantage over an American program that was dogged by inter-service and inter-departmental rivalry leading to splitting of resources.

The formation of NASA in 1958 effectively focused the American effort and avoided all future duplication of effort. This was enhanced by President Kennedy's public affirmation of support for the space program in 1961. Sergei Korolev's illness and subsequent death in 1966 left the Soviet Union without anyone of comparable ability to bring together the different strands of the Russian effort, and the Soviet Union was never again able to directly challenge the Americans for any major space milestone. When this became apparent, the Soviet leadership became less willing to put resources in the space program. In America, even after the dramatic success of the moon landing, the lack of competition from the Soviet Union led to a loss of interest in the space race and a withdrawal of funding.

For a short time, leading the exploration of space was a matter of national pride for the two most powerful nations on Earth. This rivalry led to amazing progress in a very short time—from the launching of the very first satellite to a man stepping on to the surface of the moon in just 12 years. Without the urgency brought about by the desire of both powers to defeat the other, this would not have happened in such a short time. In general, the Cold War between America and Russia caused little but mistrust, misery, and the development of ever more destructive weapons. But in the case of the space race, it brought more progress, more rapidly than anyone could ever have imagined.

Made in the USA
Las Vegas, NV
11 September 2023

77425655R00030